Alexander Peskanov's

THE RUSSIAN TECHNICAL REGIMEN

FOR THE PIANO

(Series of Six Books)

Exercise Volume V

SCALES IN DOUBLE NOTES:
THIRDS, SIXTHS AND OCTAVES

Technical Editor - Lynn Radcliffe

W.M. Co. 11617E

W.M. Co. 11617E

To
My Beloved Teachers in Russia,
ROSALIA MOLODIETZKAYA and her son, EMIL

IN GRATEFUL REMEMBRANCE

Cover Illustration by LYNN RADCLIFFE

W.M. Co. 11617E

Concert pianist and composer, appeared as soloist with London Philharmonic, English Chamber Orchestra, National Symphony and orchestras of Baltimore, St. Louis, Houston, Utah and others. Concertized in 48 states and 20 countries on four continents. Recipient of ASCAP awards for music and theater compositions. Graduated from Stoliarsky School of Music, Odessa, Ukraine, and received Masters Degree from Julliard School of Music, New York. Married to Lu Ann, concert flutist and teacher; has two children.

ALEXANDER PESKANOV

Author

Music/piano enthusiast, retired from career in the aerospace industry. Was record reviewer for American Record Guide Magazine, artist. Graduated with BS degree from Syracuse University, 1942. Married to Jean; has two children.

LYNN E. RADCLIFFE

Technical Editor

* * * * * * * * * * * * * * * * * * *

Lynn Radcliffe and I started our relationship with a fair exchange: he told me about traveling in space and I told him about playing double thirds and broken chords. Lynn was one of the first people to whom I introduced elements of the Russian Technical Regimen for piano. Each of us added a new dimension to the other's life, and we found that we shared one significant quality in our characters: endless curiosity in the pursuit of knowledge. Discovering that this regimen is just as effective for a person of sixty-eight and beyond as it is for a child of ten has inspired us to write this series of books for students of all ages.

Alexander Peskanov

FOREWORD

This exercise volume is part of a series of books entitled *The Russian Technical Regimen for the Piano*. It consists of the INTRODUCTION AND GUIDE to the regimen and five exercise volumes. The Russian Technical Regimen encompasses all the technical requirements which have been in use in Russian and Soviet music schools and conservatories for more than a century.

This exercise volume presents:
1) the 24 double-thirds scales in the Russian pattern with transitions
2) the double-thirds (minor) chromatic scale in the Russian pattern
3) the 24 double-sixths scales in parallel motion with transitions
4) the Peskanov double-sixths chromatic scale in the Russian pattern
5) the 24 double-octave scales (two octaves in parallel motion) with transitions
6) the 24 double broken octave scales (two octaves in parallel motion) with transitions

The only way to achieve the understanding and the required skills for these exercises in to study the entire Part Four, Chapters VII through XIV in the INTRODUCTION AND GUIDE. All the exercises in this volume are presented in close approximation to the requirements in the Russian schools. The double-thirds scale, played in the Russian pattern, is my own modification as opposed to playing four octaves in parallel motion. The same is true for the double-thirds and double-sixths chromatic scales. The double-sixths chromatic scale is a rare specimen in any regimen. It should be pointed out that the idea of playing all twenty-four scales in double-thirds and double-sixths as continuous exercises originated as I was practicing and becoming sufficiently competent to play them all at once. As a recommendation, I advise pianists to practice double-note scales (thirds, sixths, and octaves) individually, and gradually work into practicing in groups of scales with transitions. The ultimate goal in being able to play from C to C (the great voyage through all twenty-four keys).

In all phases of *The Russian Technical Regimen for the Piano* accents must always be the foundation for the rhythm and points of relaxation. The benefits of the Regimen can accrue only if it is practiced in the proper manner with full realization of the Guide Book instructions.

Alexander Peskanov

Supplementary materials and additional teaching aids include:

Introduction and Guide ("Guide Book")

Exercise Volume I, Scales in Single Notes

Exercise Volume II, Broken Chords

Exercise Volume III, Russian Broken Chords

Exercise Volume IV, Arpeggios and Block Chords

Exercise Volume V, Scales in Double Notes: Thirds, Sixths, Octaves

Instructional Videos, "In Search of Sound"
Produced by Classical Video Concepts, Inc.

Piano Olympics Kit, Manual and Demonstration Video
Produced by CVC, Inc.

Piano Video Exchange, Presented by the Baldwin Piano
and Organ Co. and CVC, Inc.

DOUBLE–THIRDS SCALES
IN TWENTY–FOUR KEYS
(Russian Pattern)

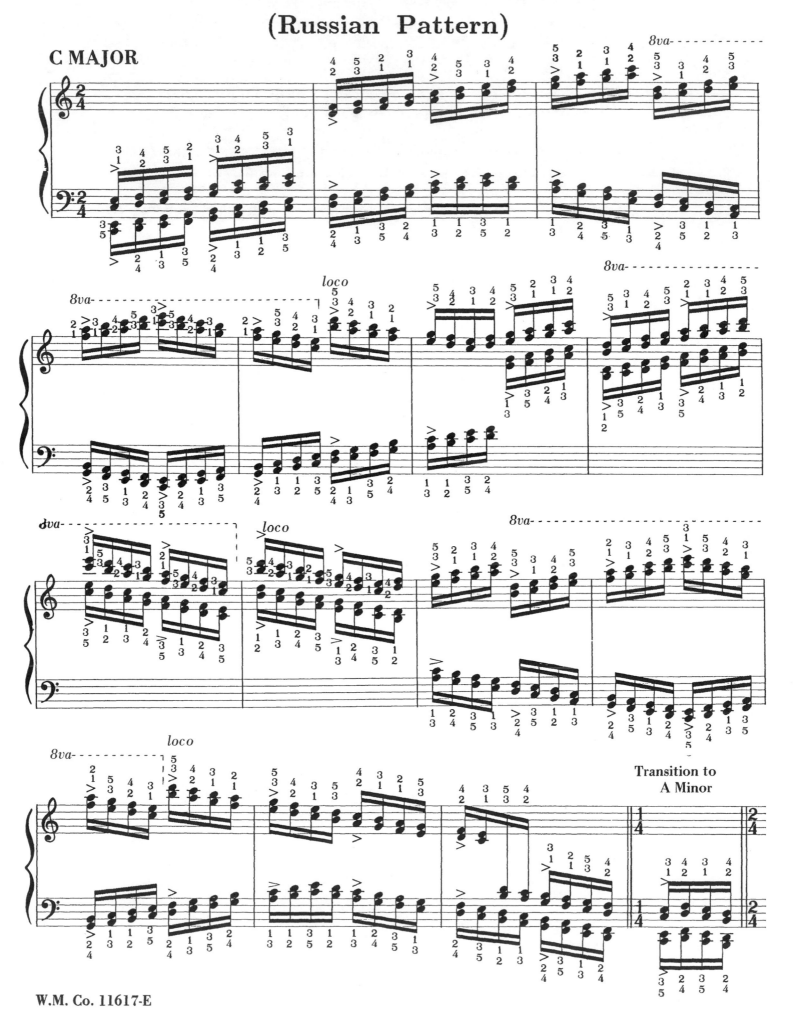

A MINOR

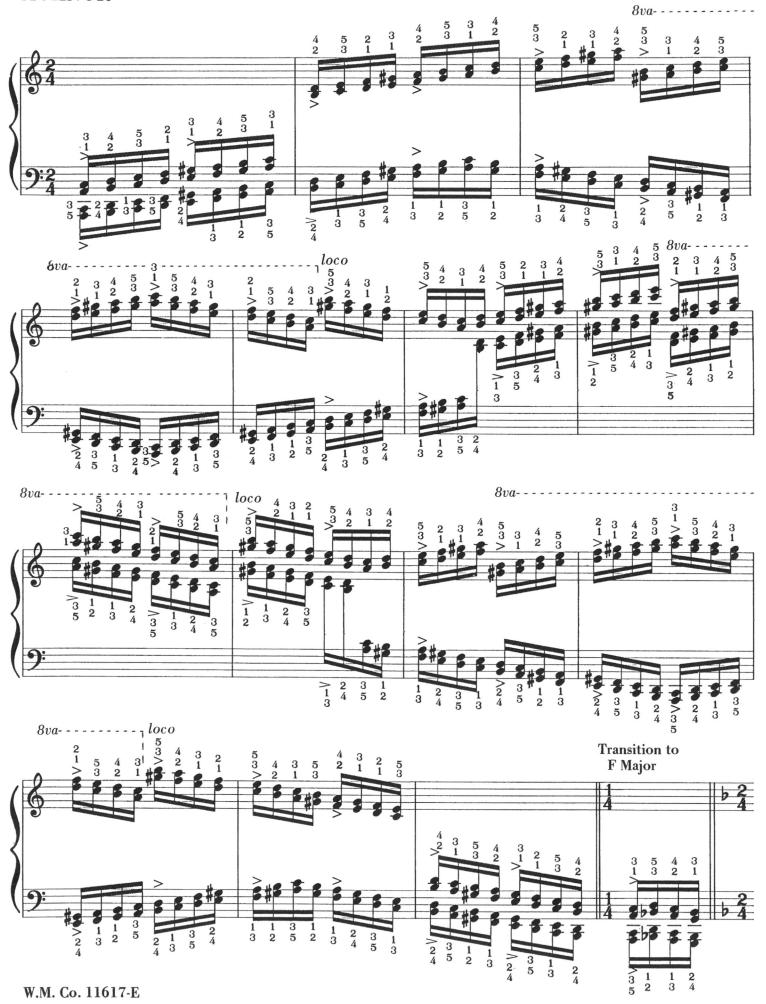

F MAJOR

Transition to D Minor

D MINOR

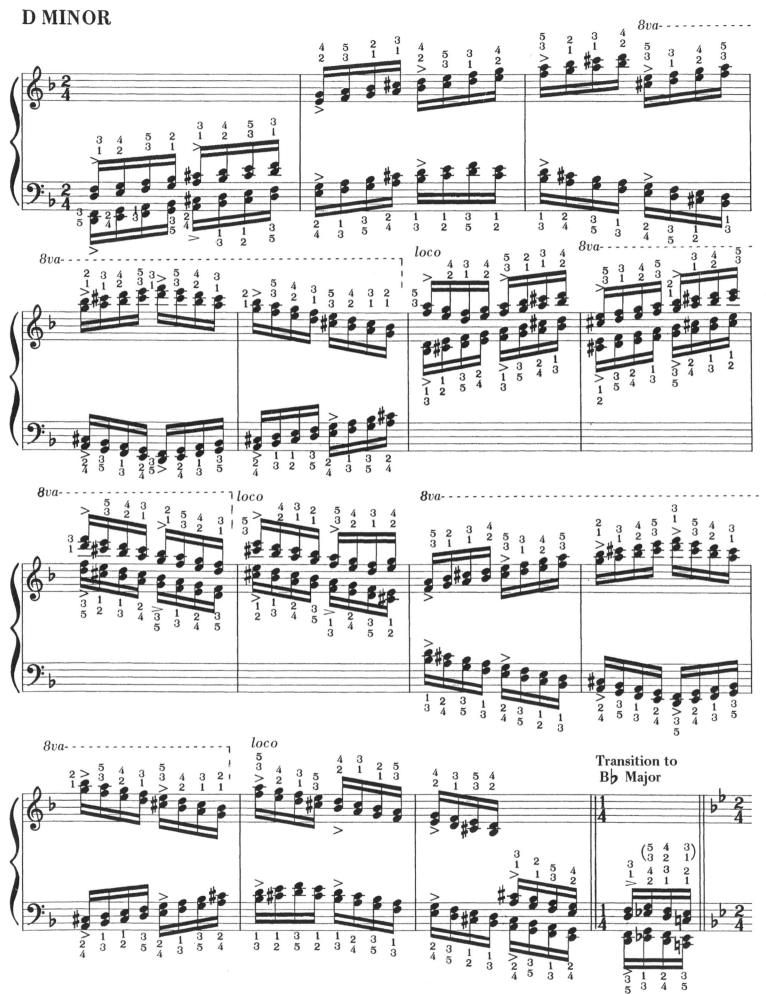

B♭ MAJOR

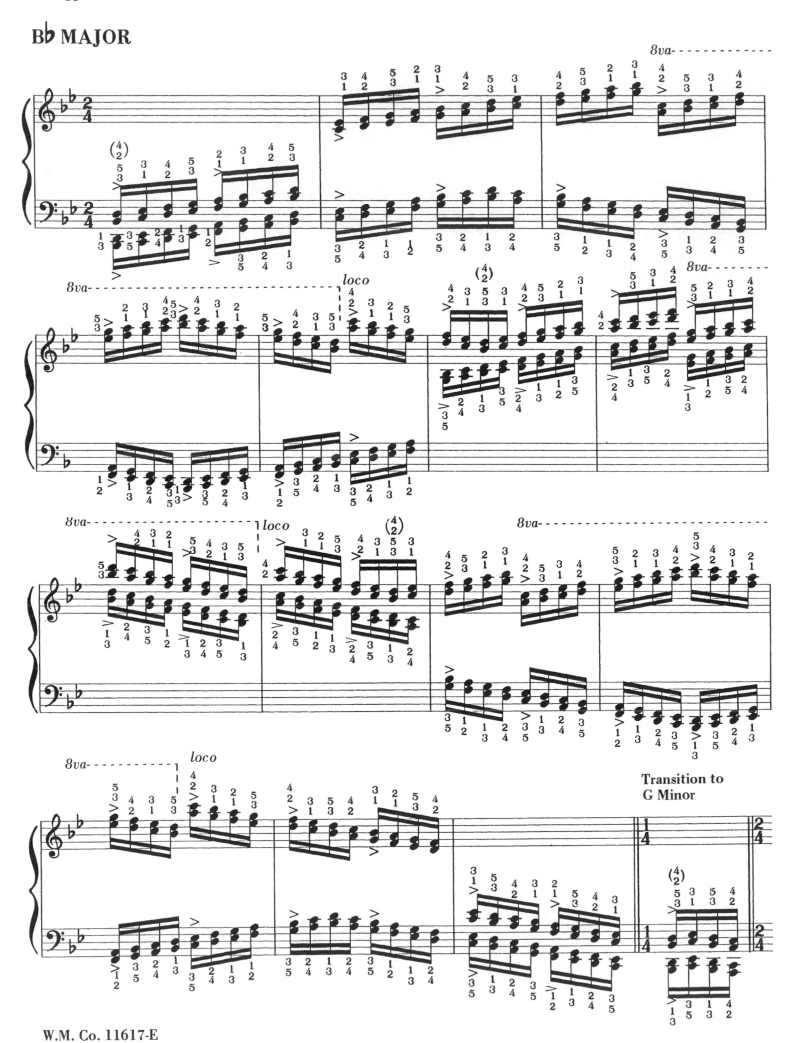

Transition to
G Minor

G MINOR

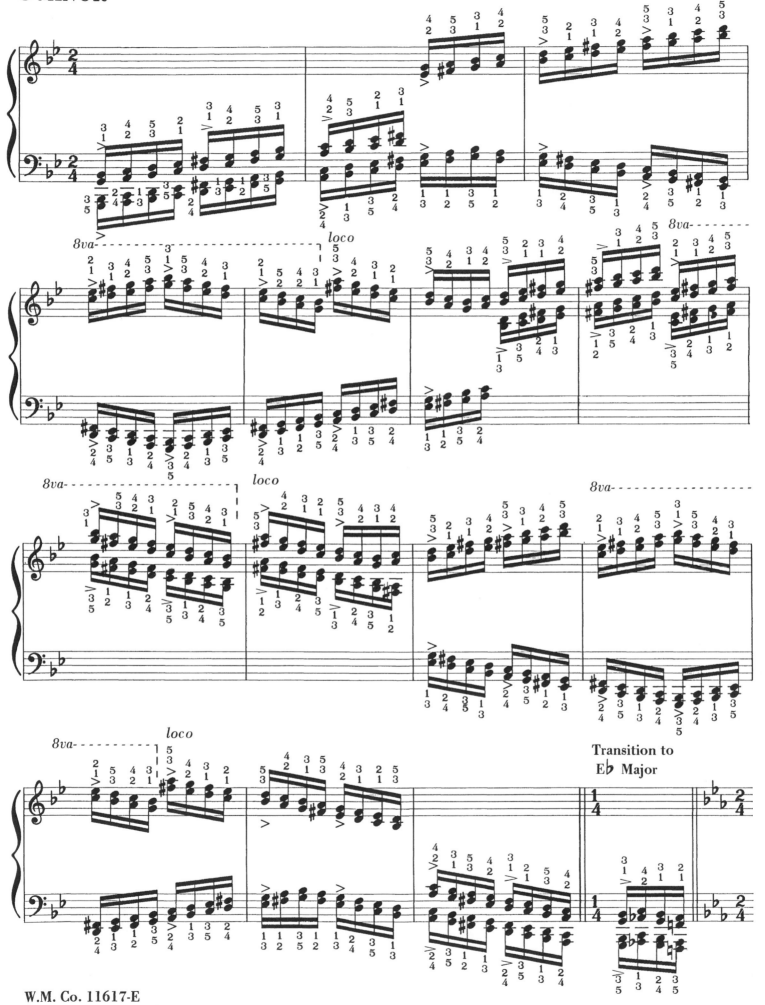

Transition to
E♭ Major

E♭ MAJOR

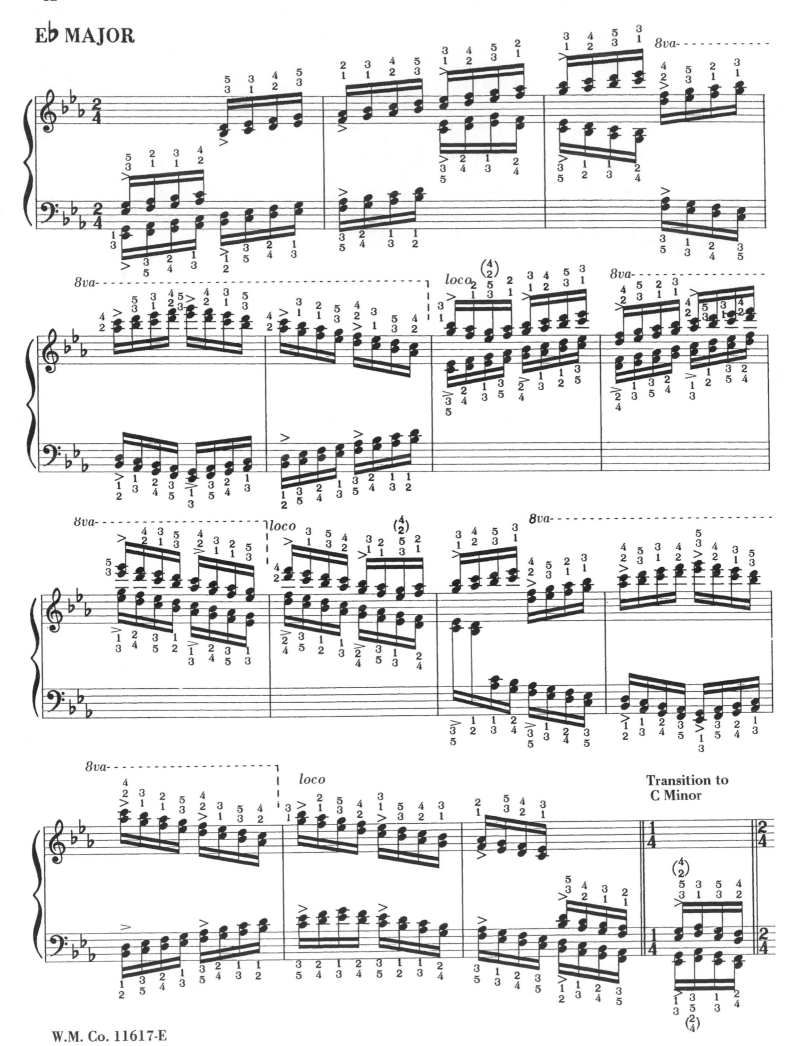

Transition to
C Minor

C MINOR

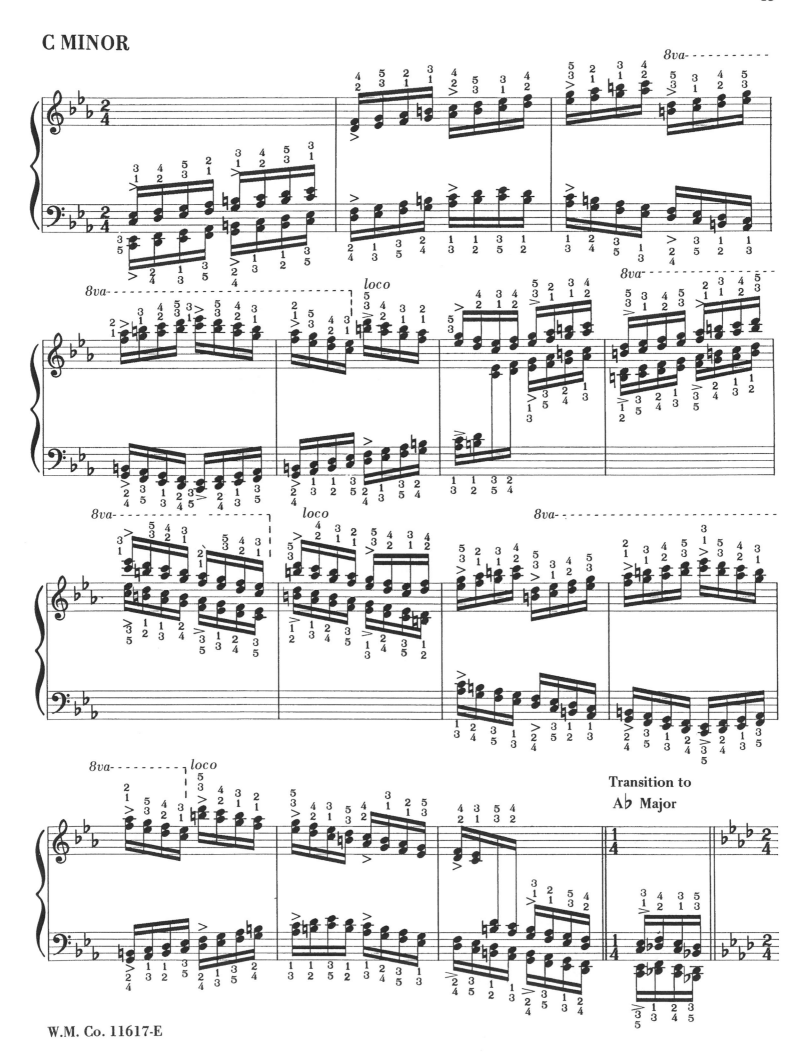

Transition to
A♭ Major

Ab MAJOR

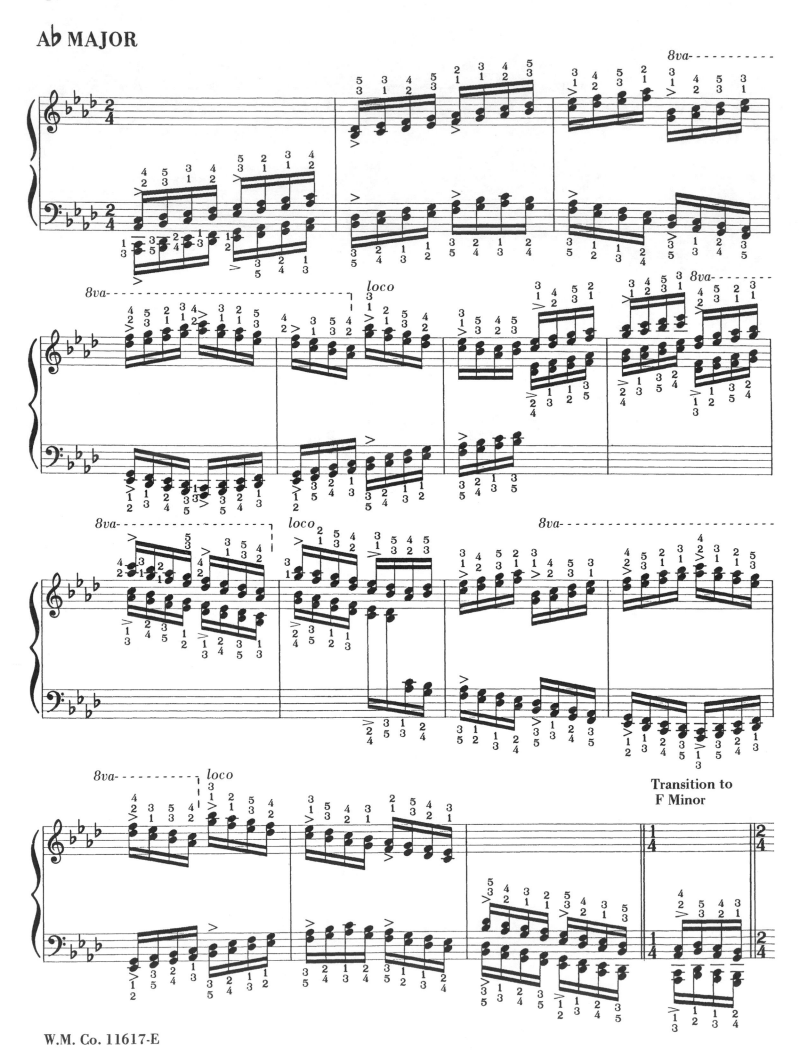

Transition to F Minor

F MINOR

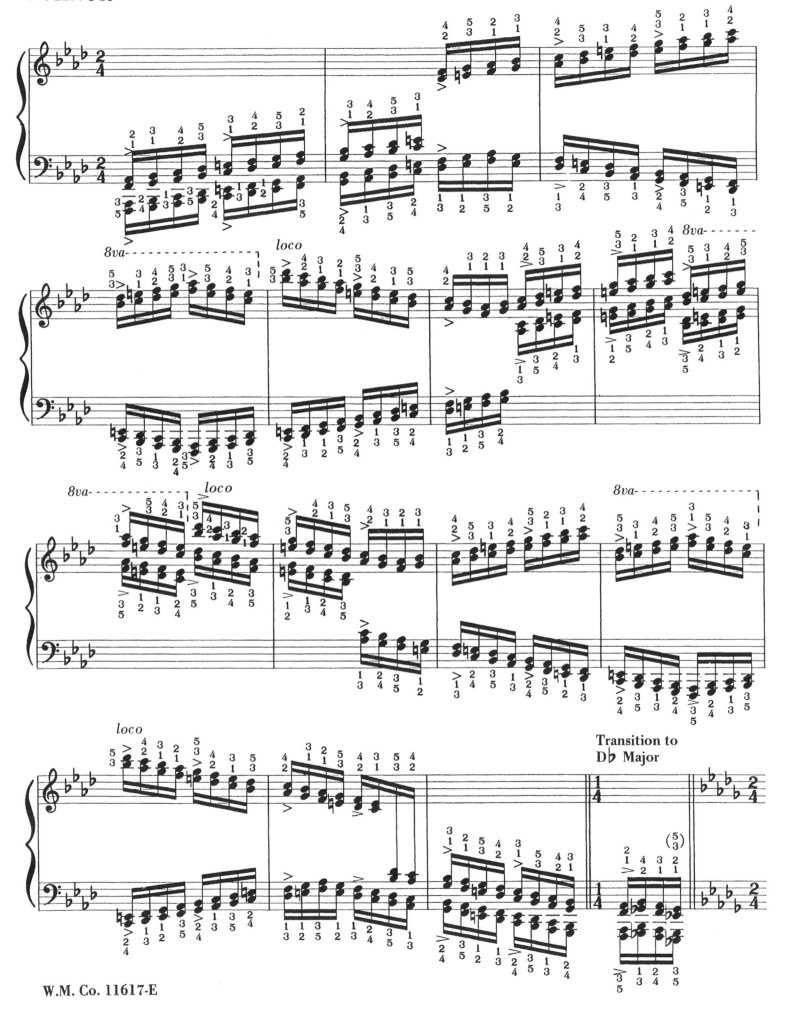

D♭ MAJOR

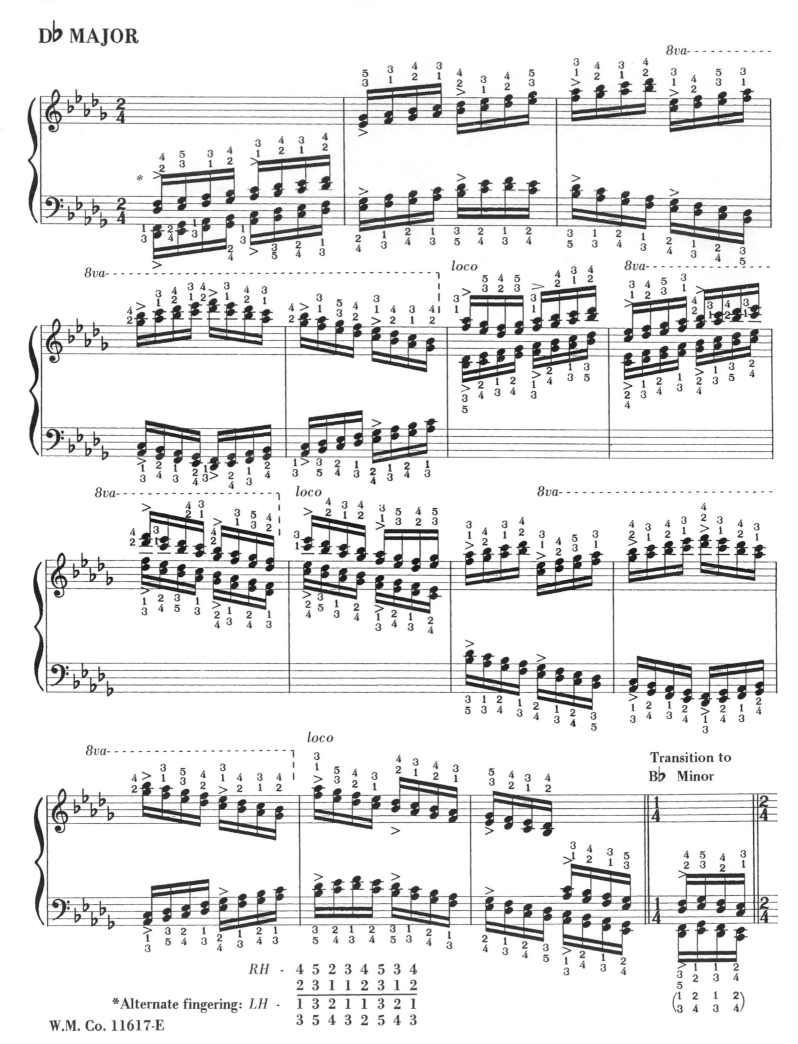

B♭ MINOR

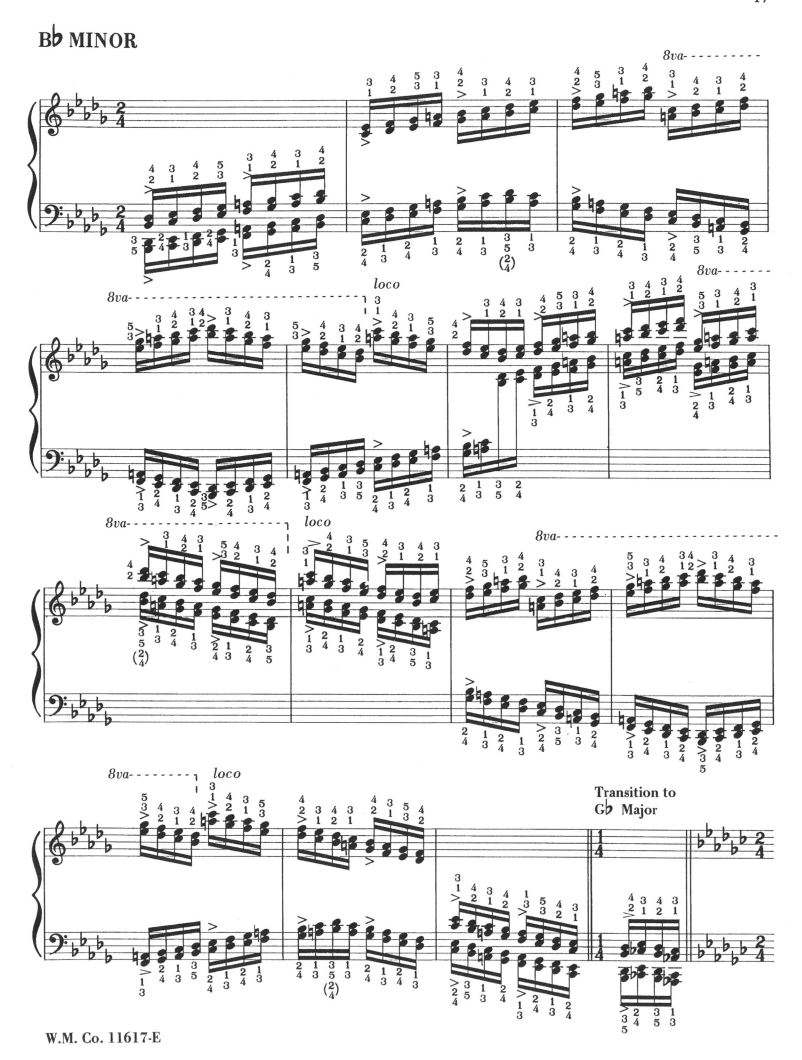

G♭ MAJOR

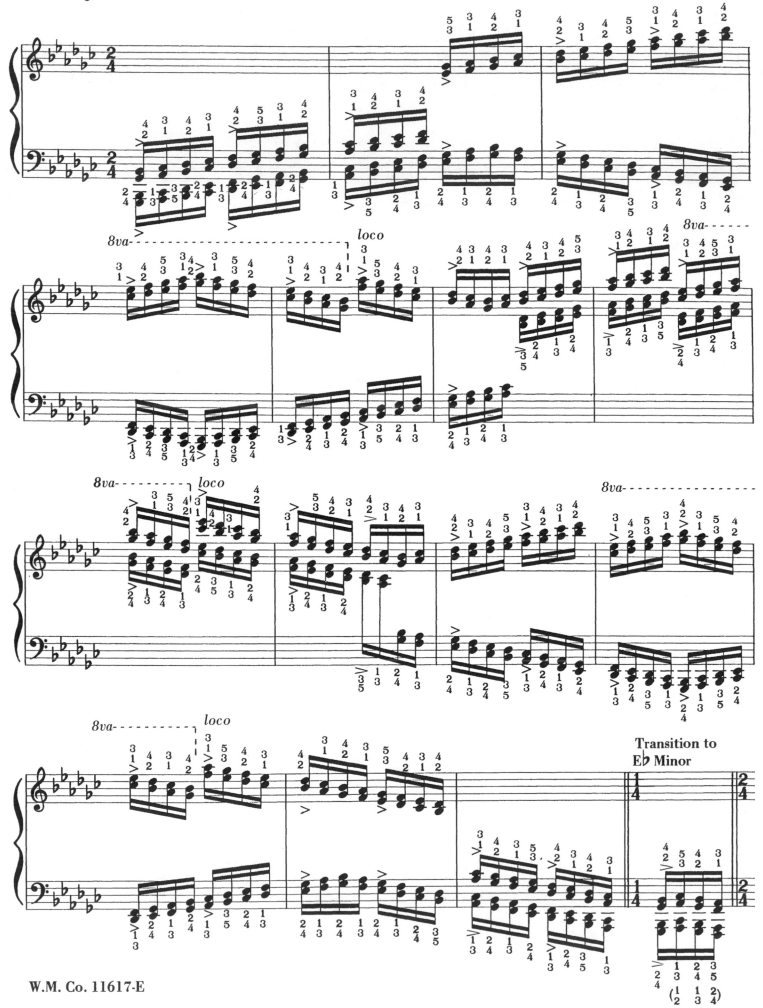

E♭ MINOR

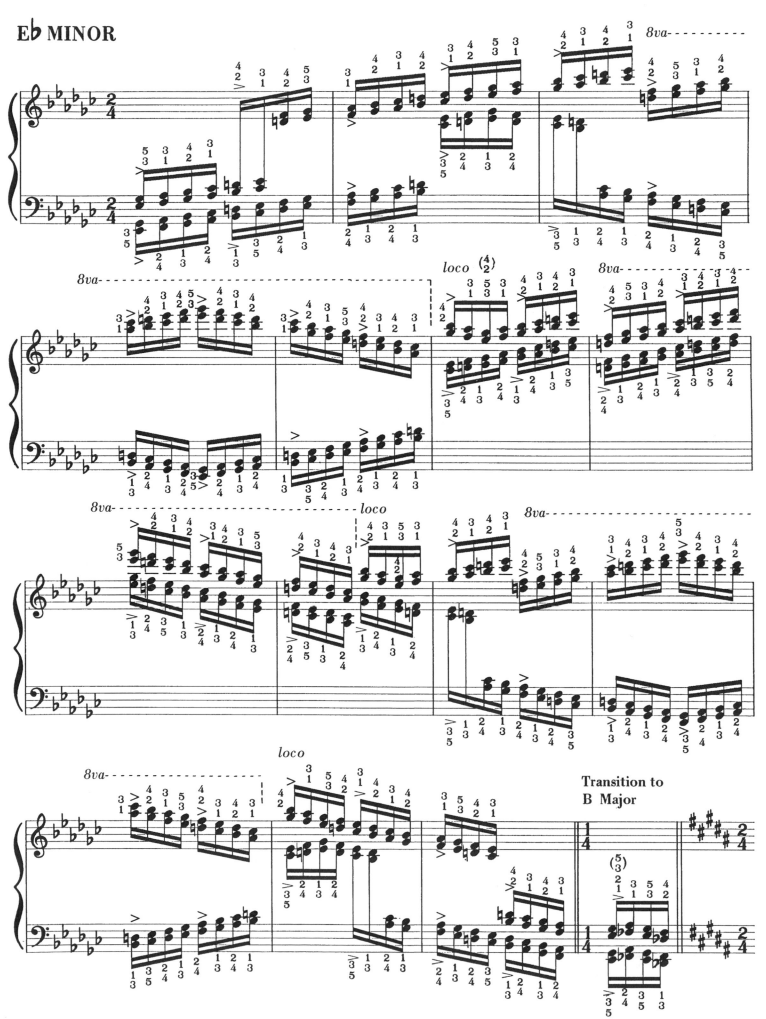

B MAJOR

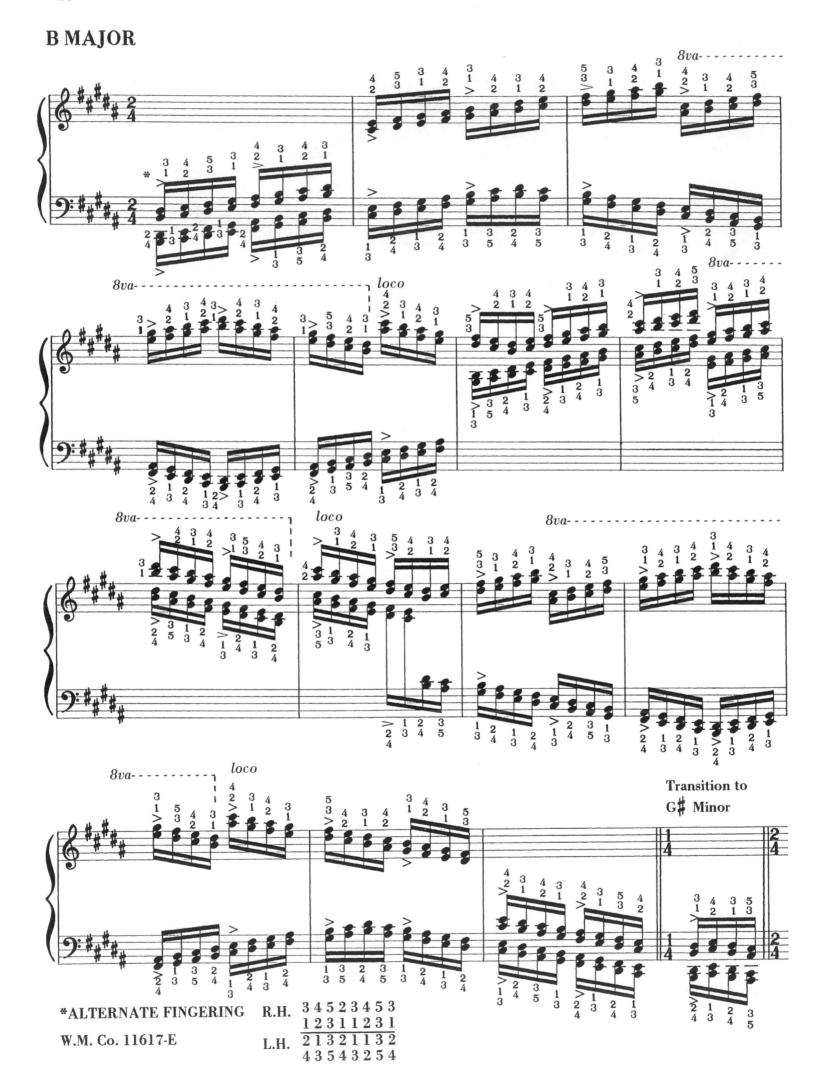

ALTERNATE FINGERING

R.H.	3 4 5 2 3 4 5 3	
	1 2 3 1 1 2 3 1	
L.H.	2 1 3 2 1 1 3 2	
	4 3 5 4 3 2 5 4	

Transition to G♯ Minor

G♯ MINOR

Transition to E Major

E MAJOR

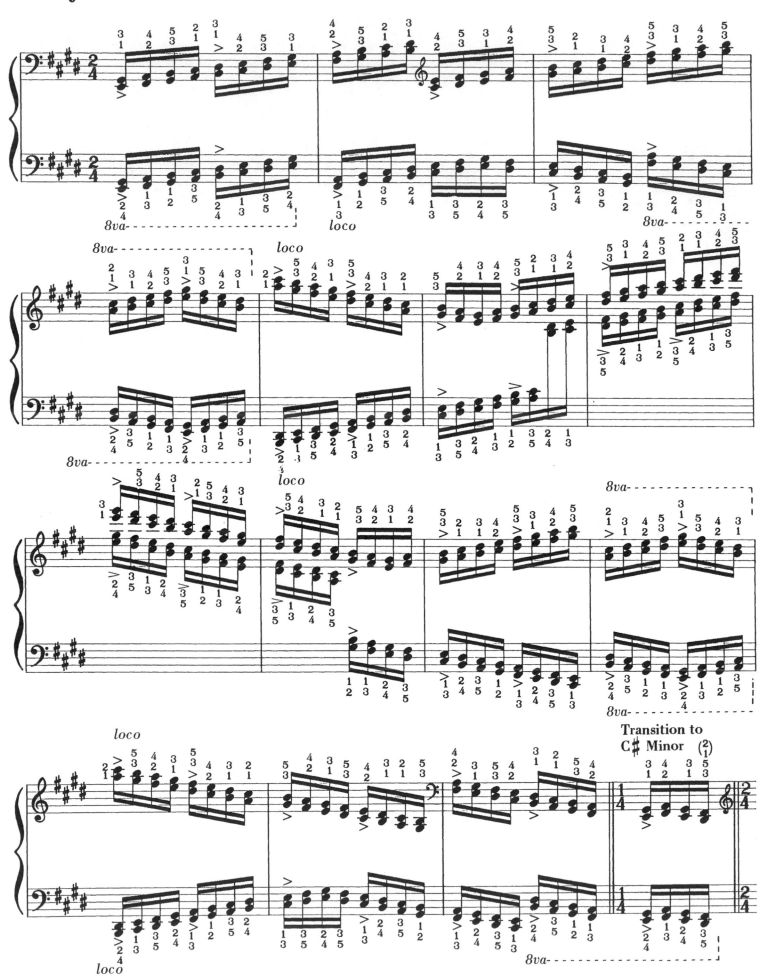

C# MINOR

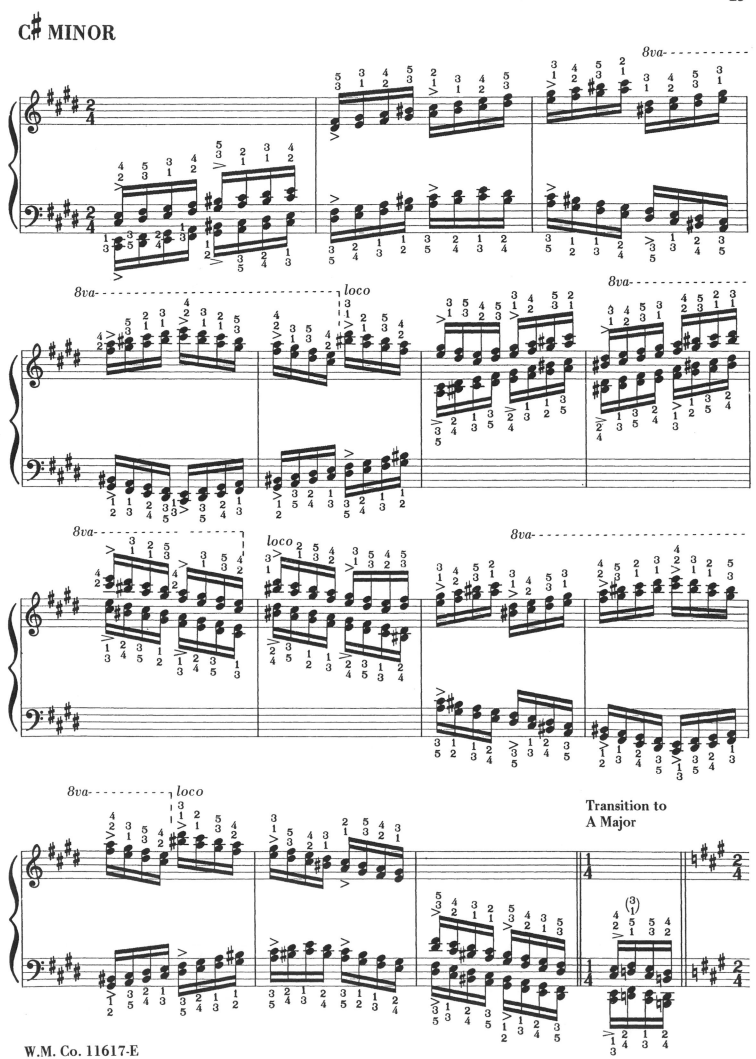

Transition to
A Major

A MAJOR

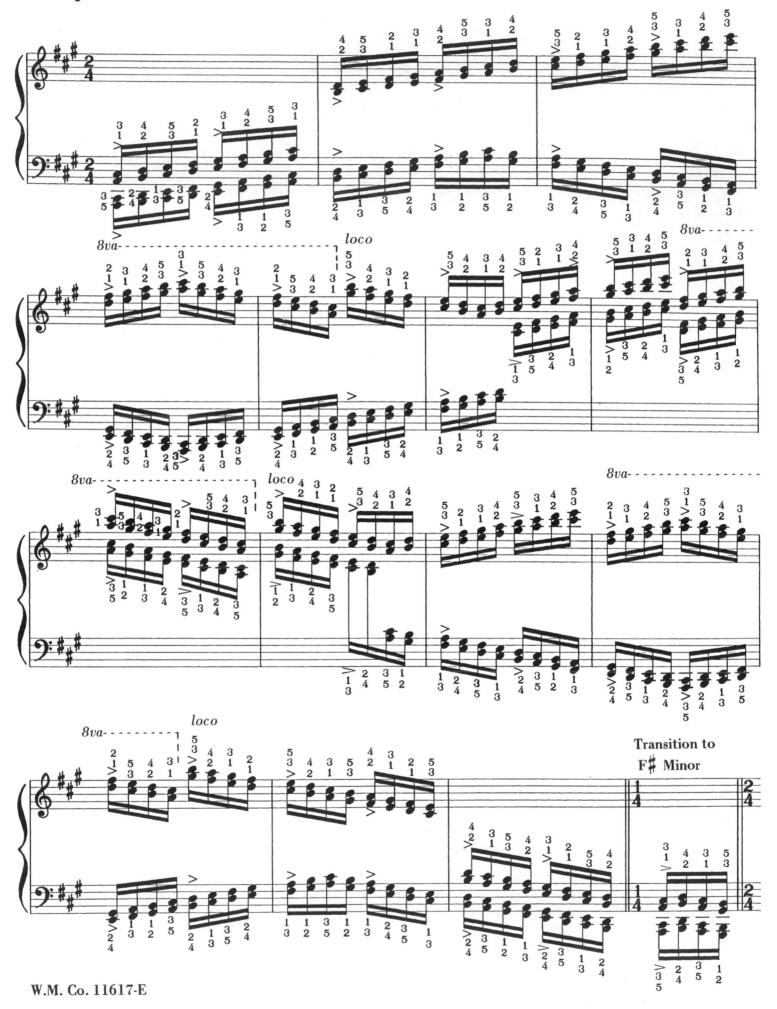

F# MINOR

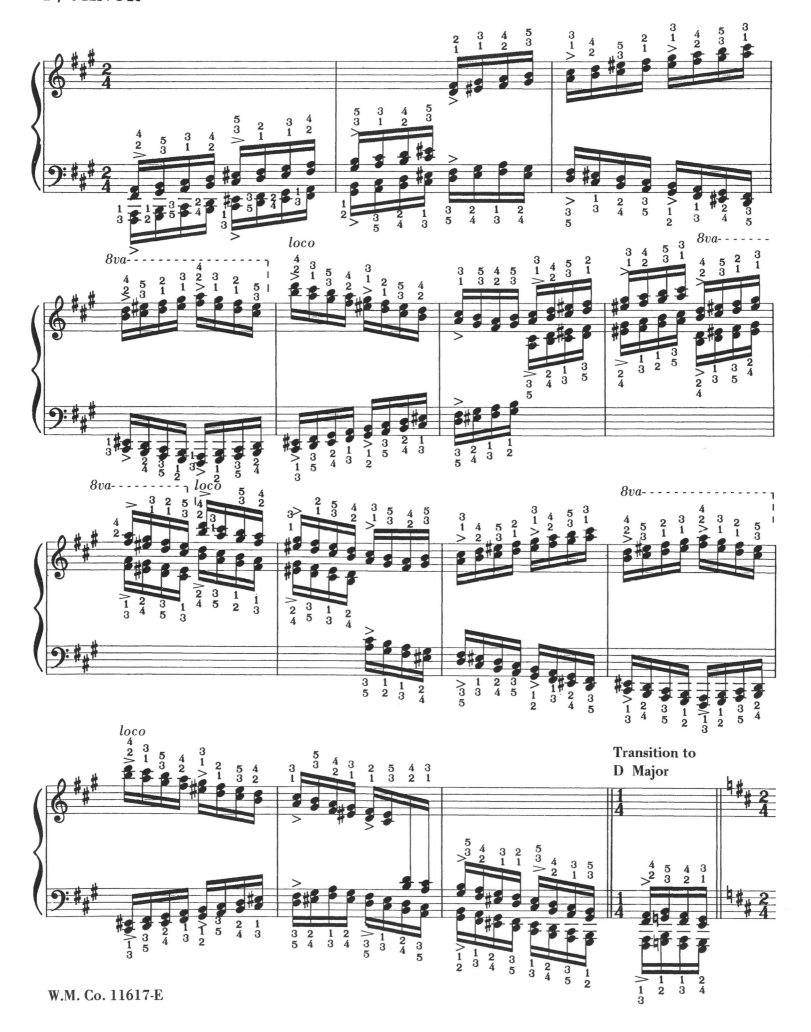

Transition to D Major

D MAJOR

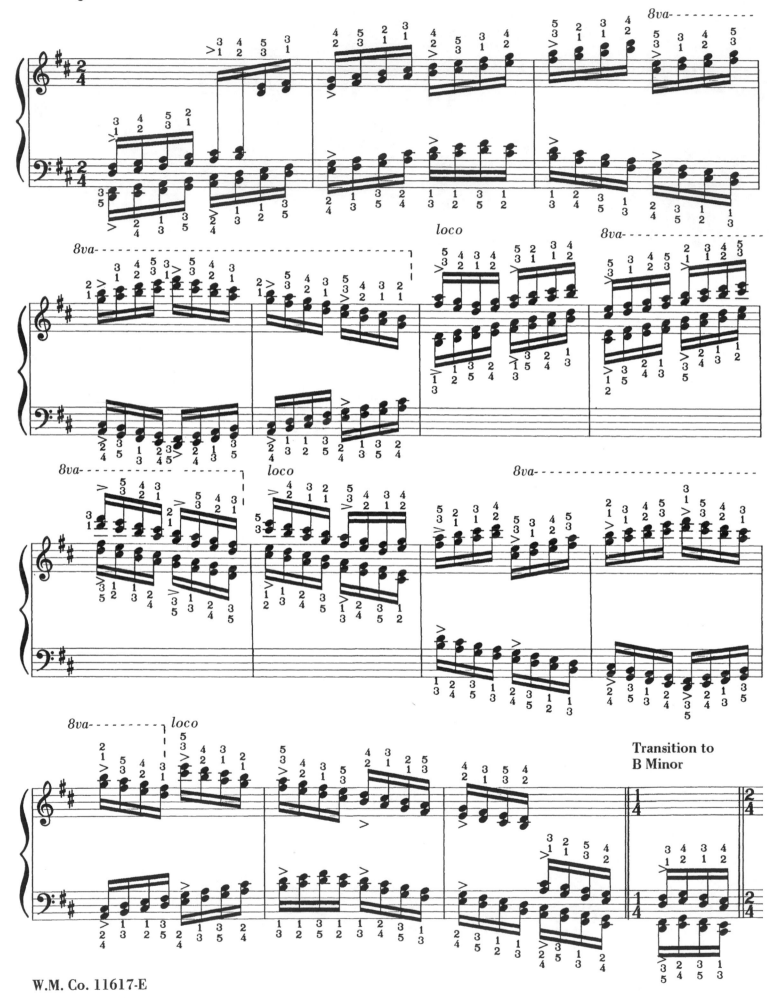

B MINOR

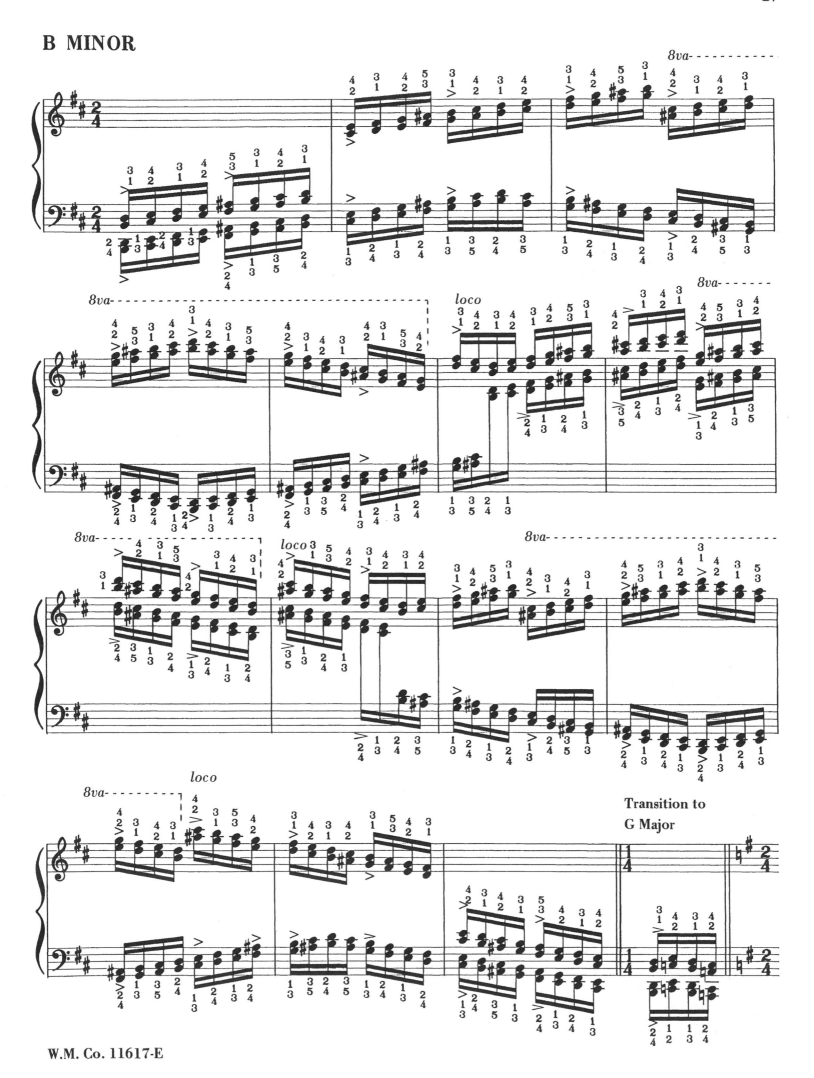

Transition to G Major

G MAJOR

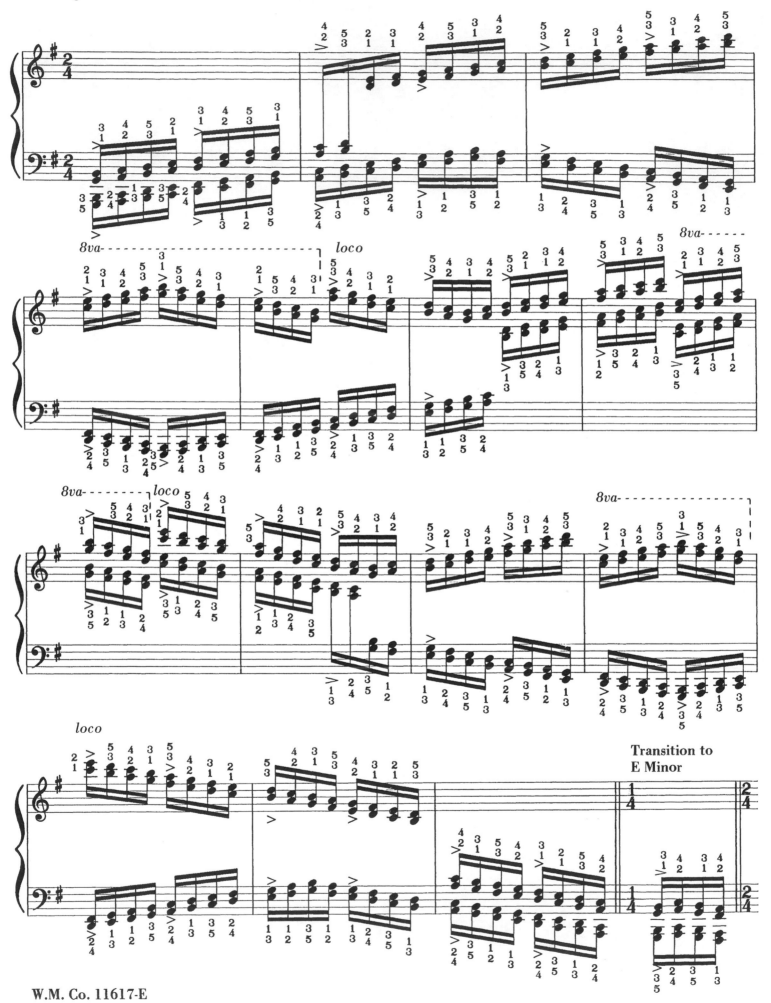

E MINOR

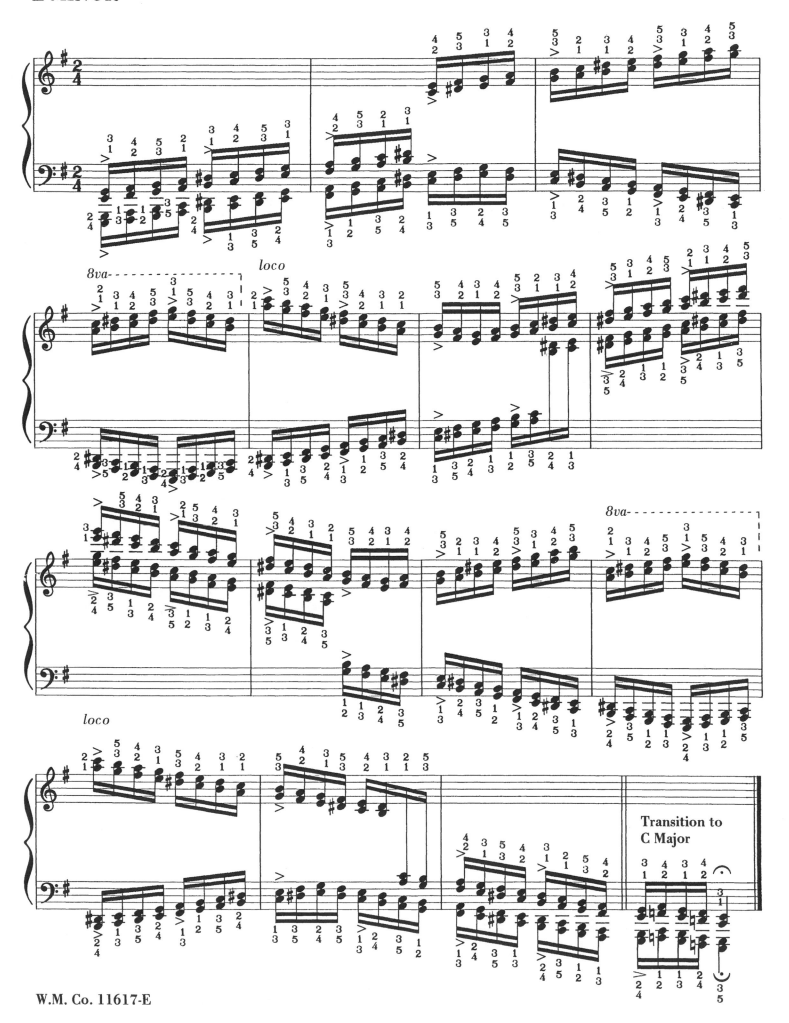

DOUBLE SIXTHS SCALES,
IN THE TWENTY-FOUR KEYS

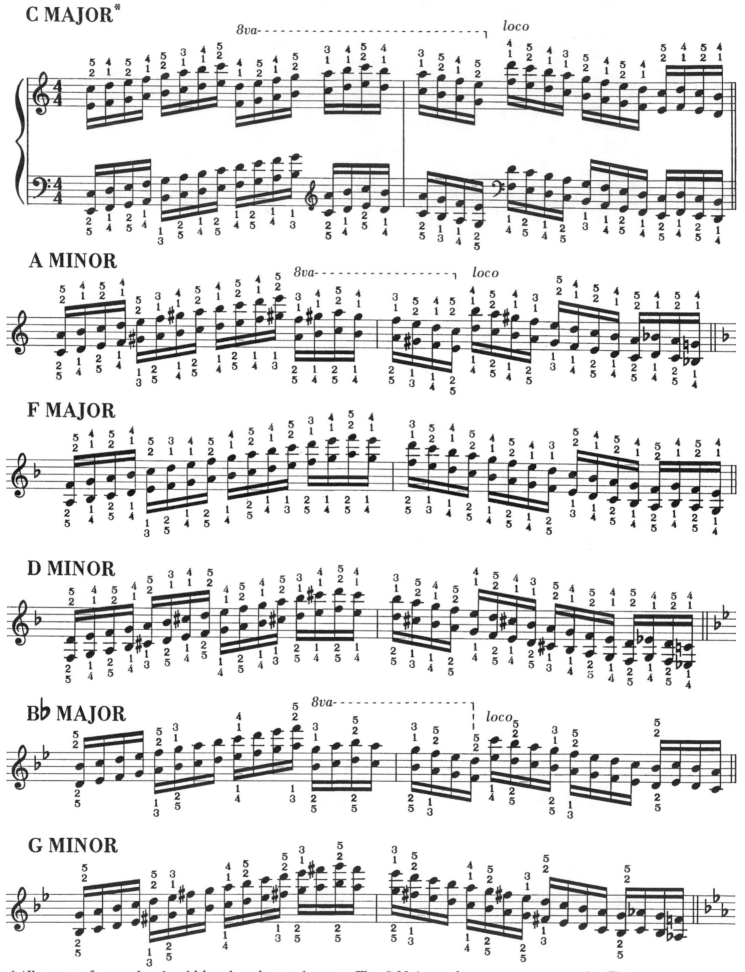

All twenty four scales should be played a tenth apart. The C Major scale serves as an example. This presentation of double sixth scales produces a much richer sonority than playing them one octave apart. This is the author's preference. It should be noted that the fingering is identical for all 24 scales.

W.M. Co. 11617-E

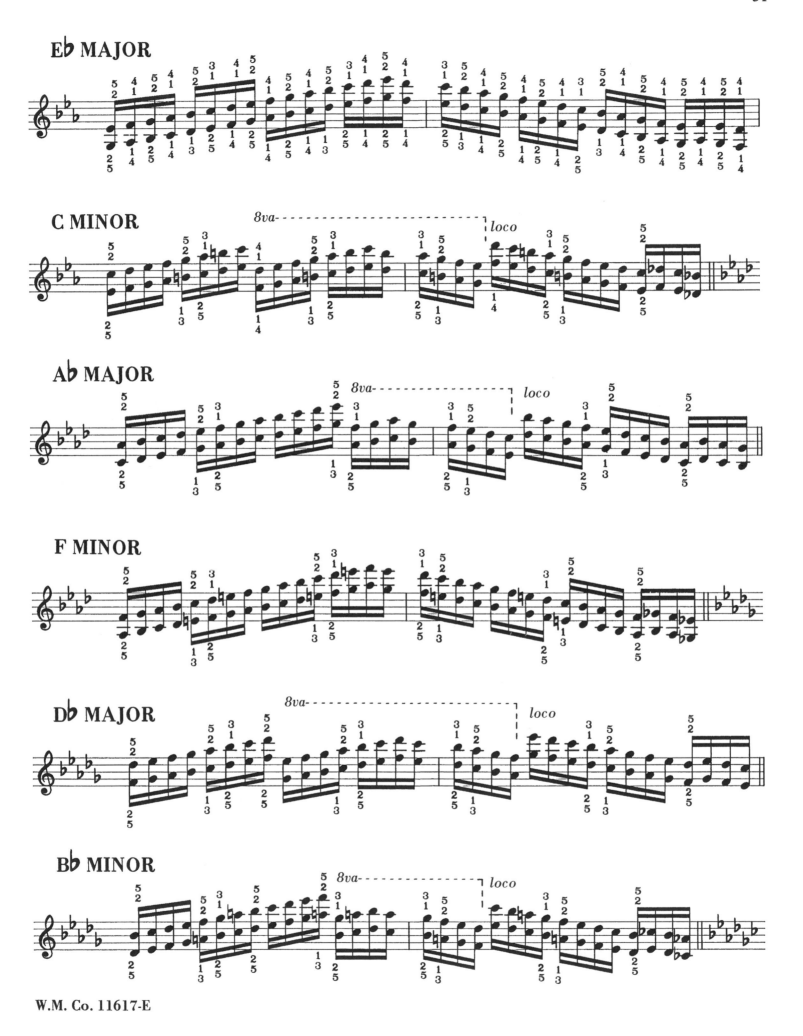

Eb MAJOR

C MINOR

Ab MAJOR

F MINOR

Db MAJOR

Bb MINOR

W.M. Co. 11617-E

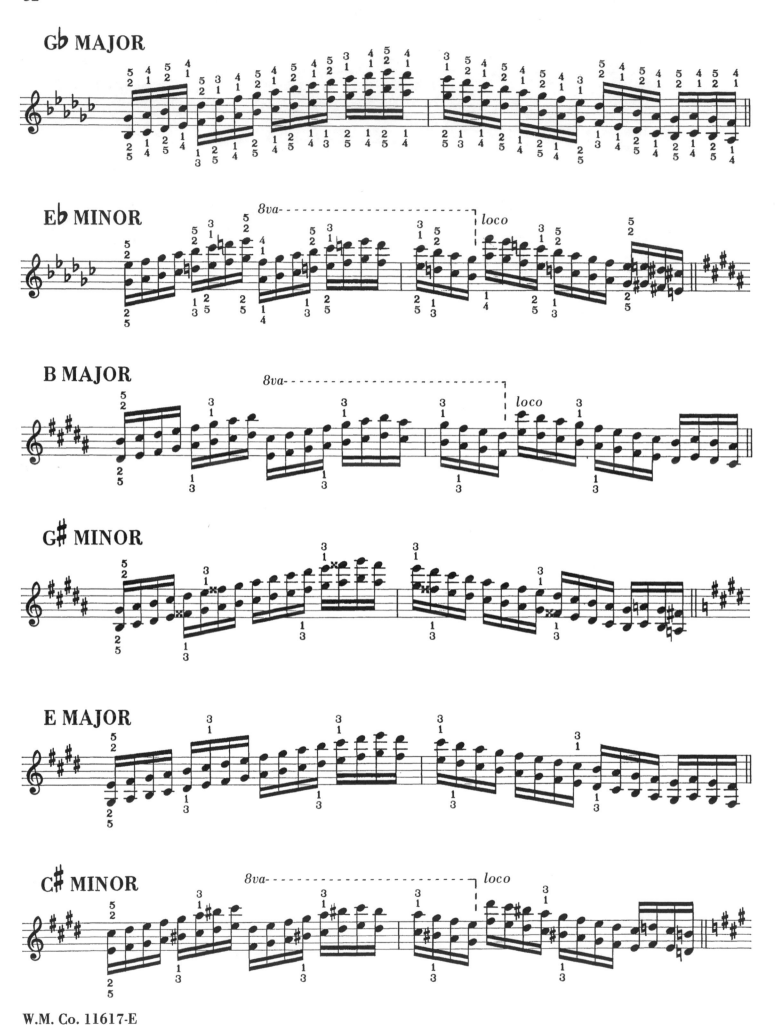

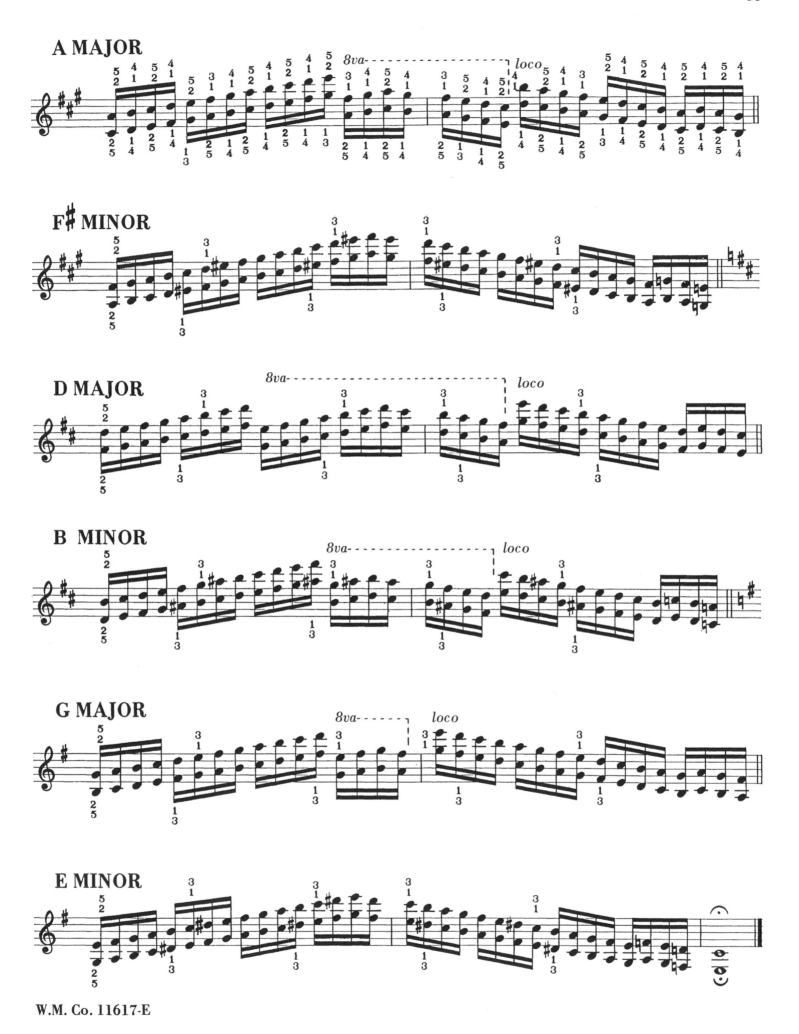

W.M. Co. 11617-E

DOUBLE THIRDS (MINOR)
CHROMATIC SCALE

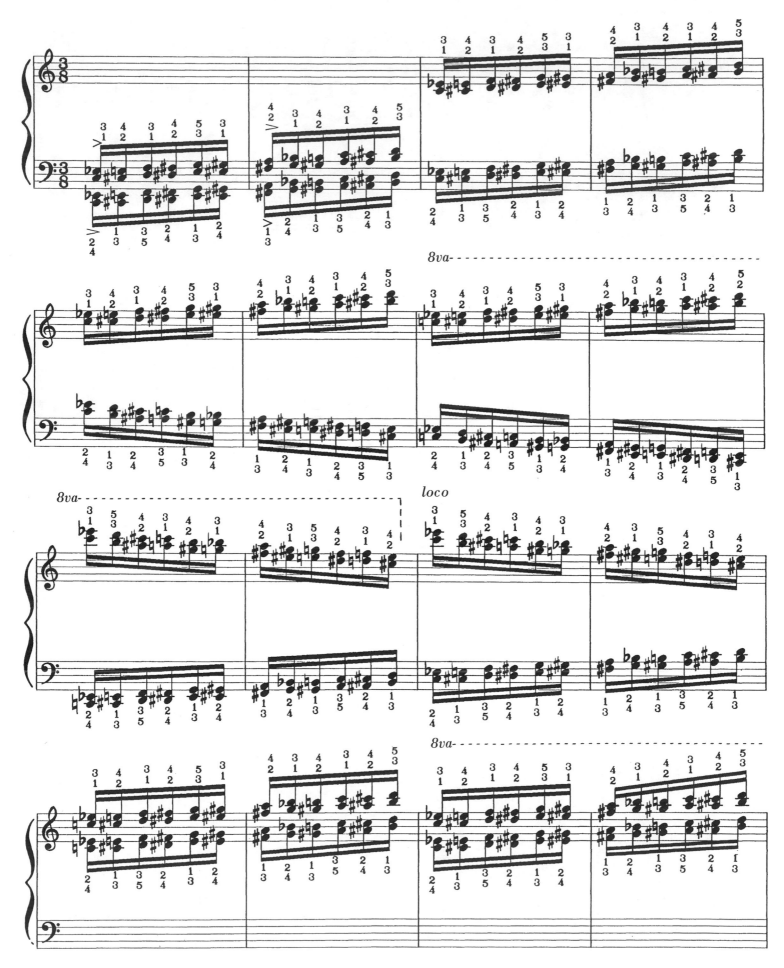

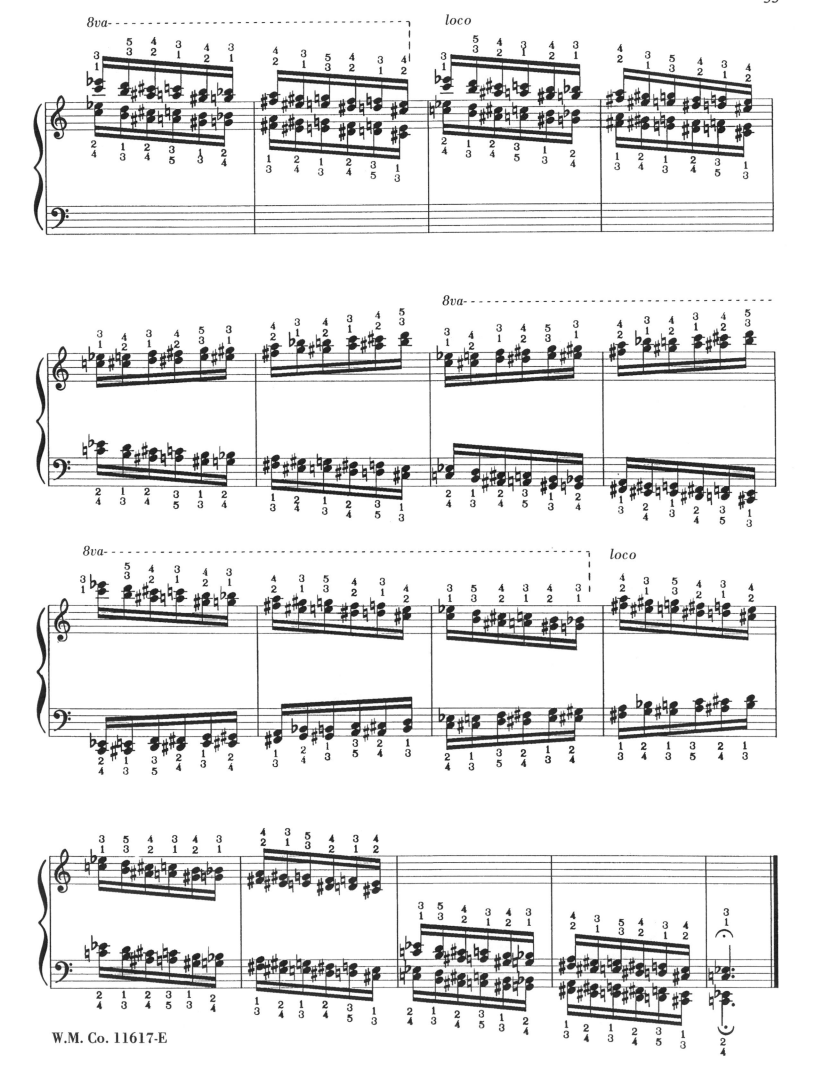

PESKANOV'S DOUBLE SIXTHS (MINOR)
Chromatic Scale in Russian Pattern

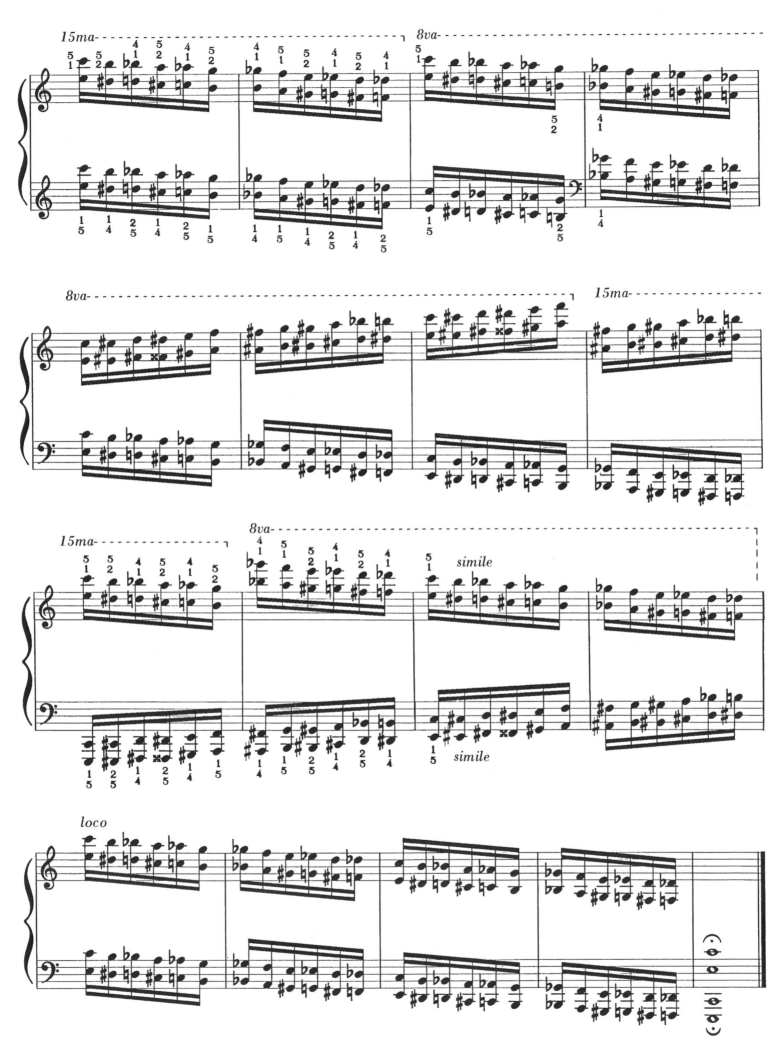

SCALES IN OCTAVES
IN THE TWENTY–FOUR KEYS *

(Use Fourth Finger on Black Notes)

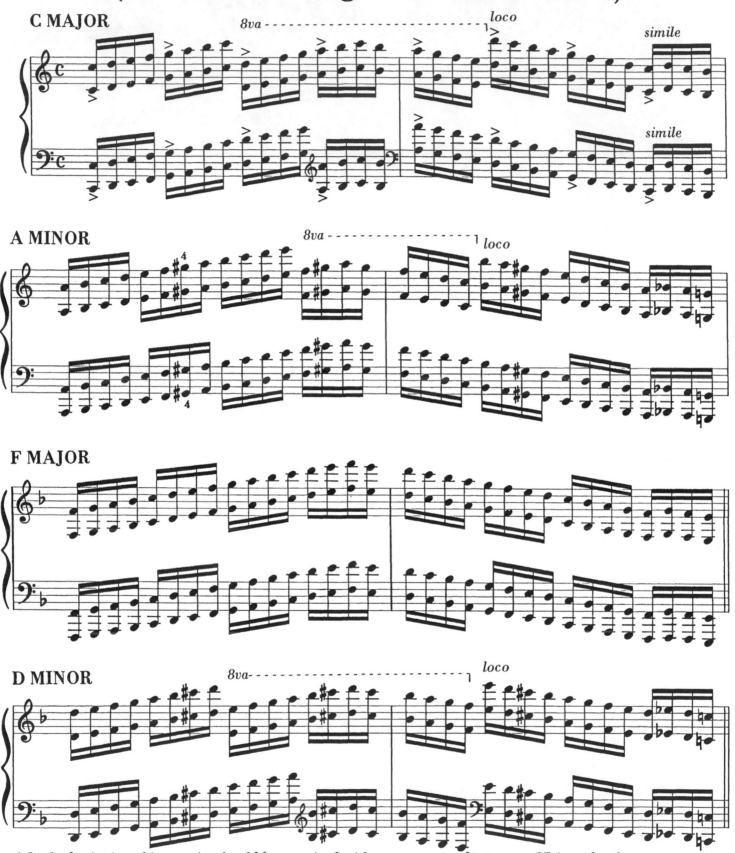

C MAJOR

A MINOR

F MAJOR

D MINOR

* In the beginning, this exercise should be practiced with accents every four notes. Ultimately, the accents will come on the the first note of each group of eight.

W.M. Co. 11617-E

8va - ⌐

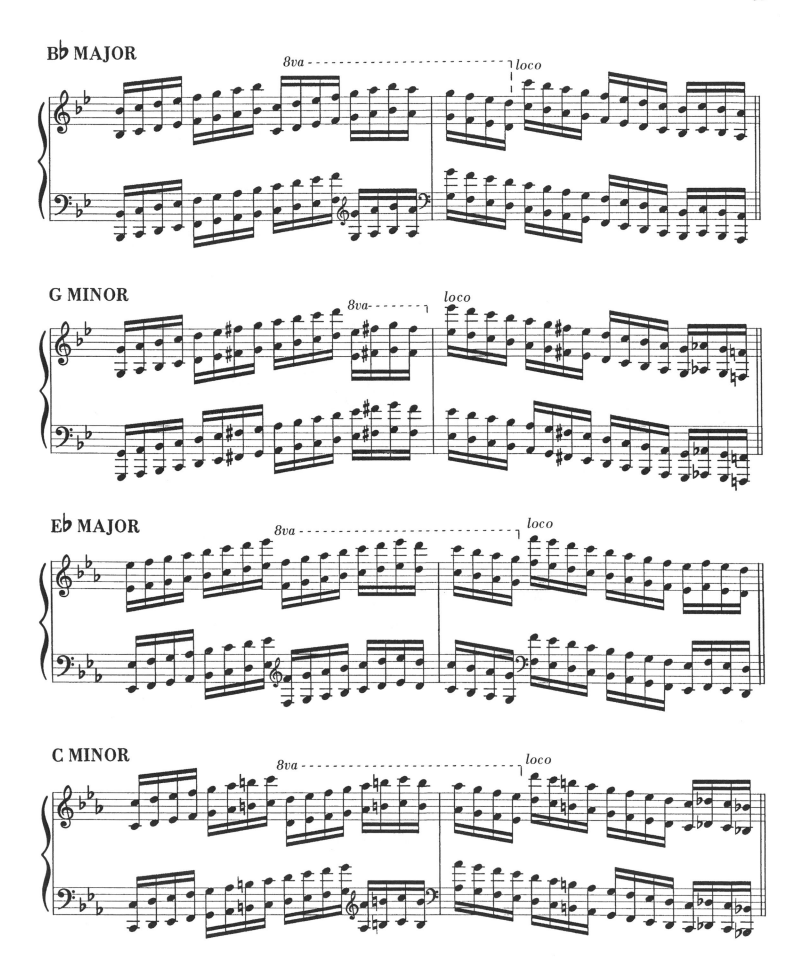

Ab MAJOR

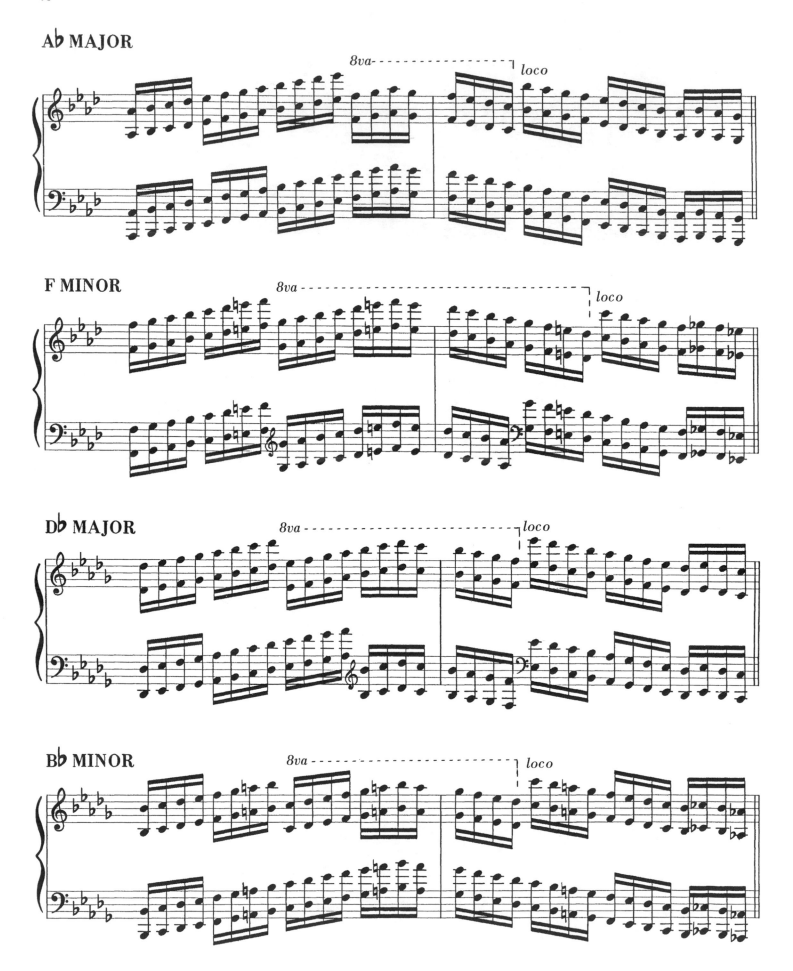

F MINOR

Db MAJOR

Bb MINOR

W.M. Co. 11617-E

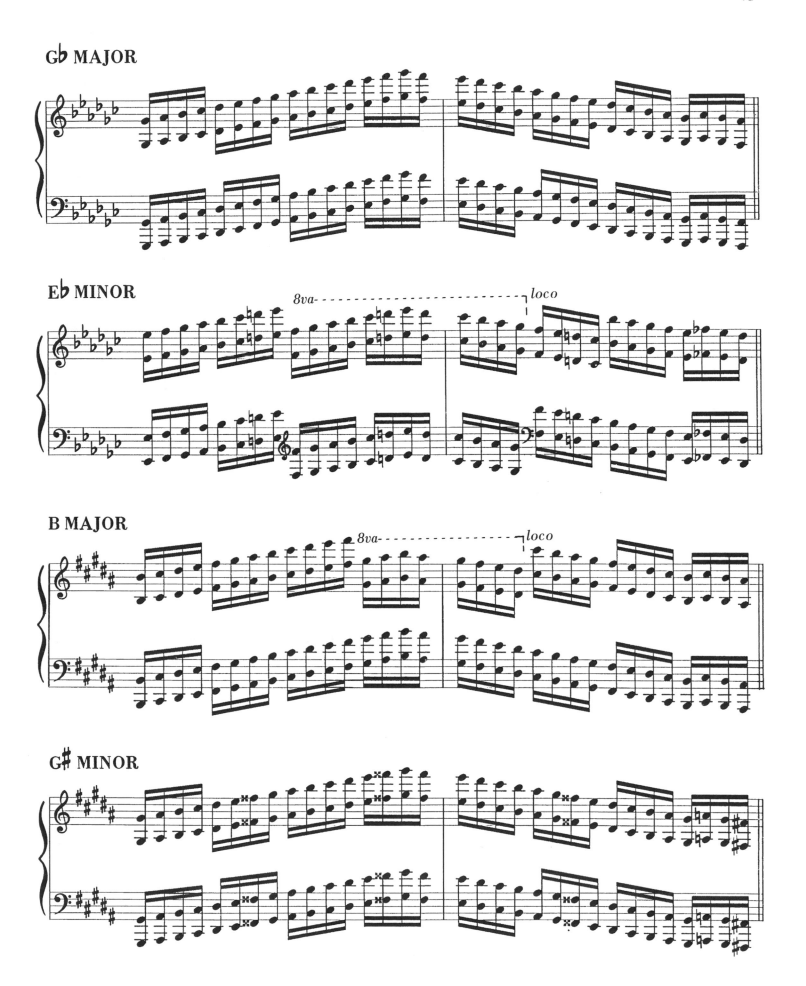

42

E MAJOR

C# MINOR

A MAJOR

F# MINOR

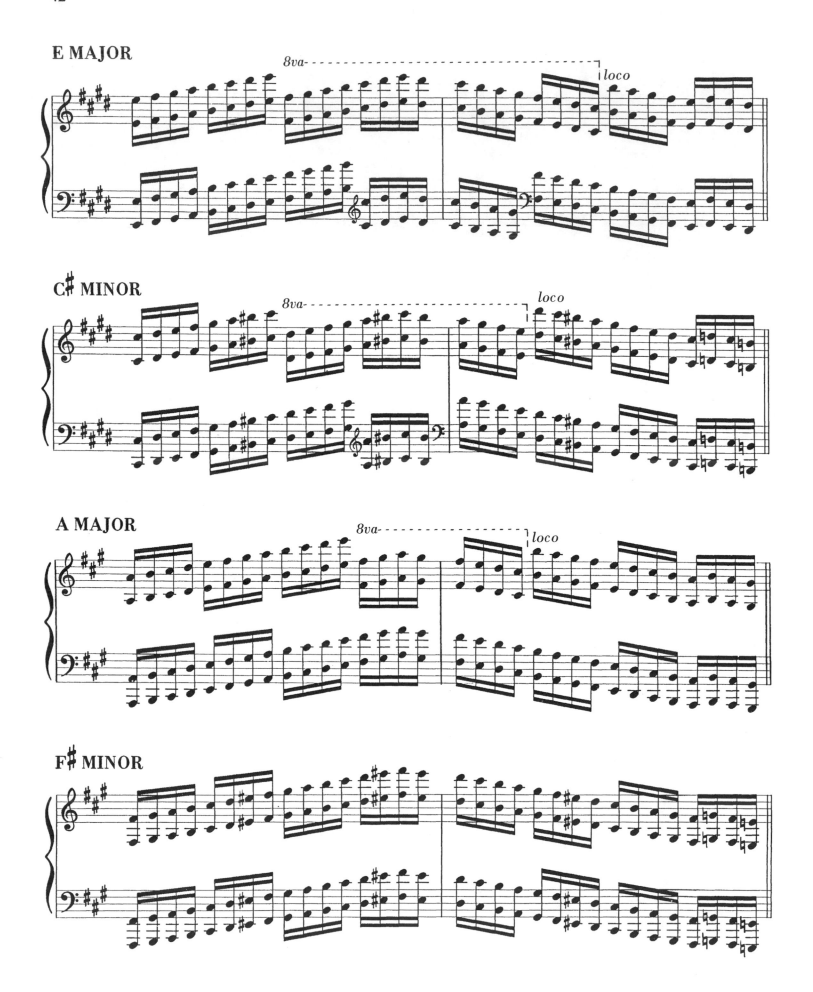

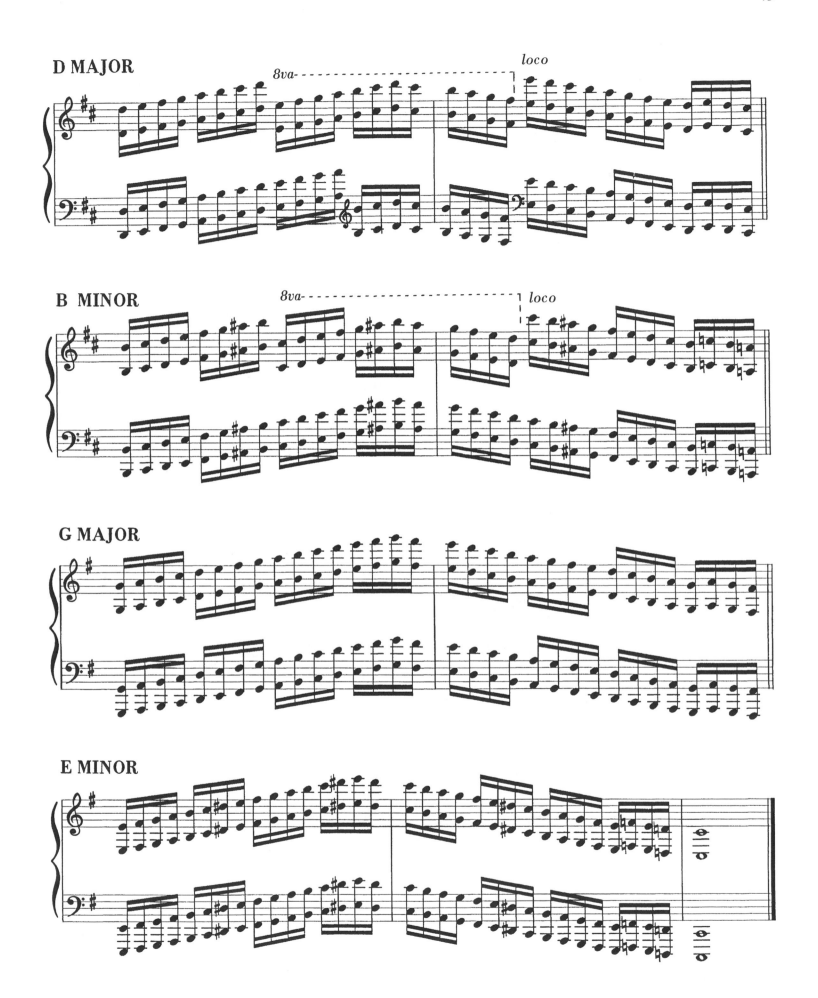

D MAJOR

B MINOR

G MAJOR

E MINOR

W.M. Co. 11617-E

SCALES IN BROKEN OCTAVES,
IN THE TWENTY–FOUR KEYS*
(Use Fourth Finger on Black Notes)

C MAJOR

A MINOR

* In the beginning this exercise should be practiced with accents every four notes. Ultimately the accents will come on the first note of each group of eight.

W.M. Co. 11617-E

F MAJOR

D MINOR

W.M. Co. 11617-E

B♭ MAJOR

G MINOR

E♭ MAJOR

C MINOR

A♭ MAJOR

F MINOR

D♭ MAJOR

B♭ MINOR

Gb MAJOR

Eb MINOR

B MAJOR

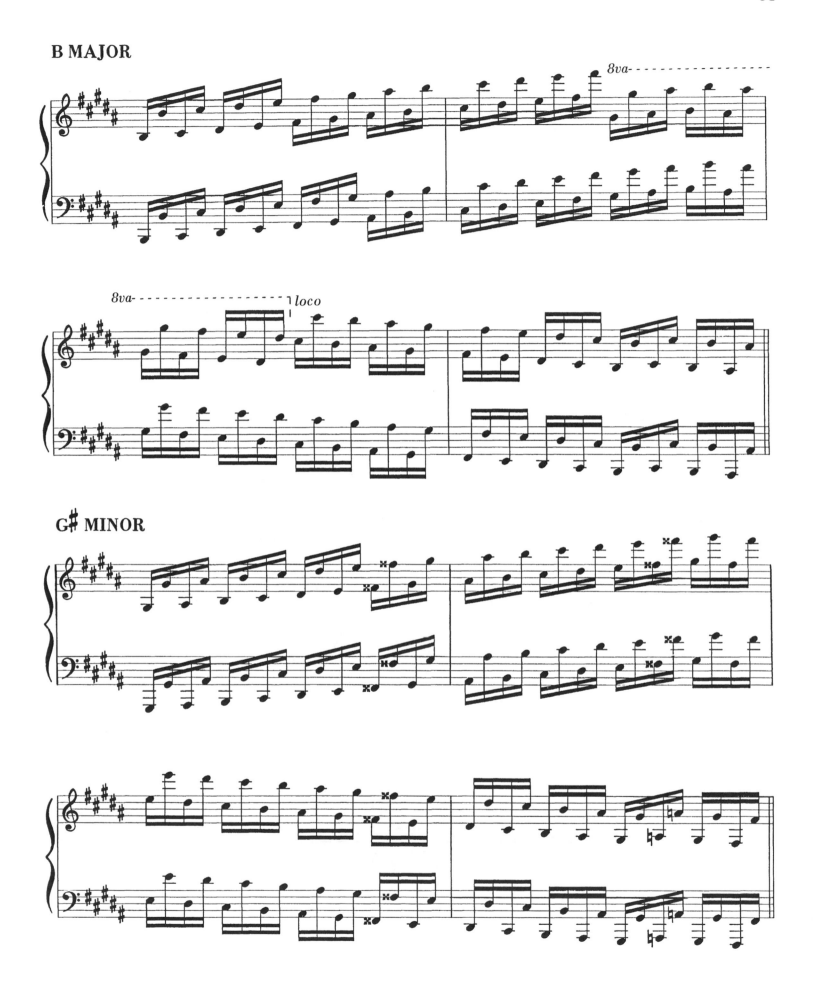

G# MINOR

E MAJOR

C# MINOR

A MAJOR

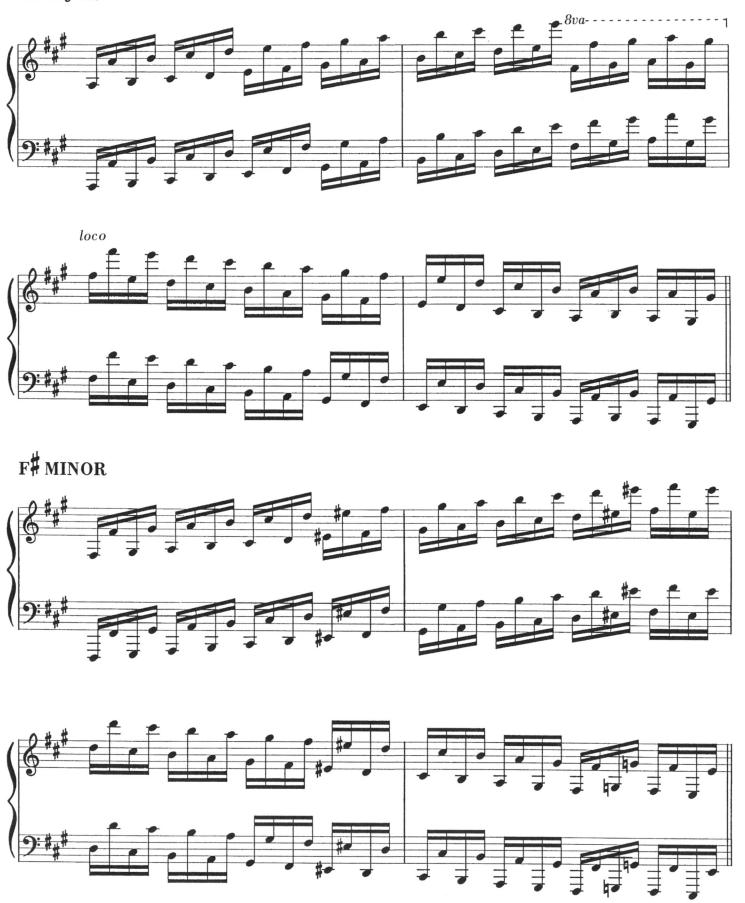

F# MINOR

D MAJOR

B MINOR

G MAJOR

E MINOR

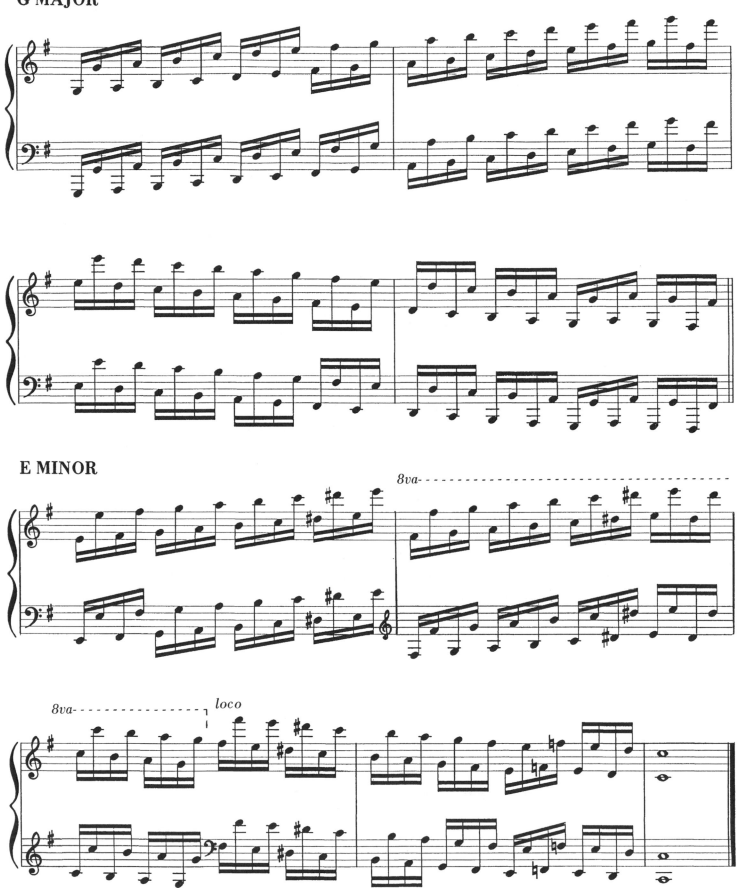

W.M. Co. 11617-E

Alexander Peskanov
On The Russian Technical Regimen

---*Introduction & Guide ("Guide Book")*

Complete instructions on how to practice the technical requirements of The Russian Technical Regimen

---*Exercise Volume I*, Scales in Single Notes

---*Exercise Volume II*, Broken Chords

---*Exercise Volume III*, Russian Broken Chords

---*Exercise Volume IV*, Arpeggios and Block Chords

---*Exercise Volume V*, Scales in Doubles Notes: thirds, sixths, and octaves

Instructional Videos, "In Search of Sound"

   Demostrations and performances by Alexander Peskanov

   (produced by Classical Video Concepts, Inc.)

---*Piano Olympics Kit* (Manual and Video)

An exciting Piano Event that helps teachers to engage students in practicing scales and exercises using the Russian Technical Regimen. Also, it offers the opportunity to demonstrate their accomplishments in the performance of their repertoire (Produced by Classical Video Concepts, Inc.)

---*The Piano Video Exchange* with Alek Peskanov

A revolutionary new way of communication between concert artist, student and artist/teacher. This personalized video program will allow the participants to make their own Video Presentation and receive a detailed critique from the artist presented by CVC Inc./Baldwin Piano and Organ Co.

W.M. Co. 11617E